Where in the World is the MOON?

Written by Molly Davis
Illustrated by Carrie Lacey Boerio

WHERE IN THE WORLD IS THE MOON?

Copyright © 2021 Mary C. Davis, Readitagain LLC, Columbus, Ohio

All rights reserved.

Library of Congress Control Number 2021921368

ISBN 9780578305585

Printed in the United States of America

Where in the World is the Moon?

Written by Molly Davis
Illustrated by Carrie Lacey Boerio

DEDICATION
For Bill,
Love you to the moon and back

1

Have you ever seen the moon rise early in the morning with a great big smile in the dark, eastern sky?

Did the moon come up
right before the sun
tippytoed
above the horizon?

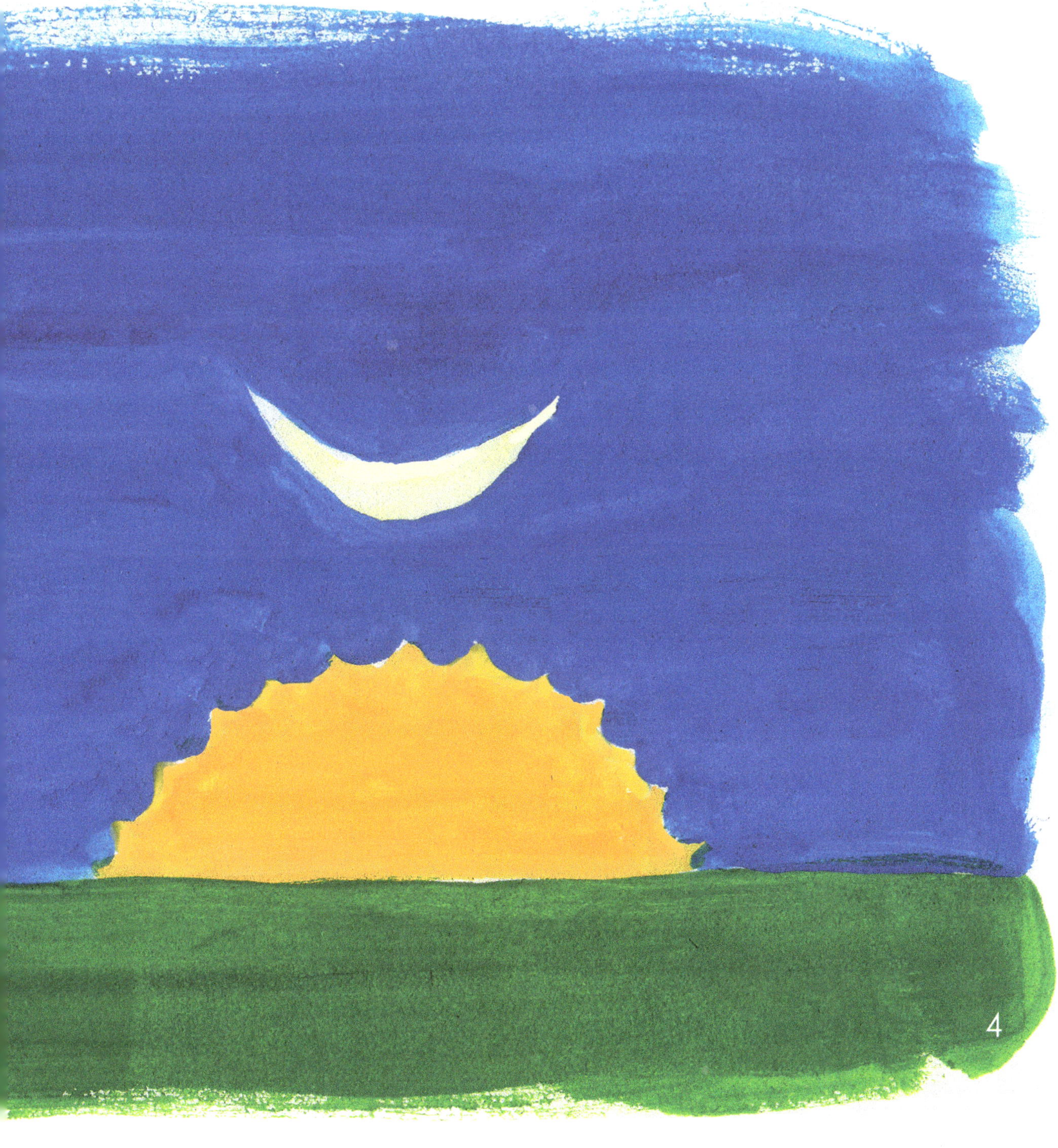

You have often seen
the moon in the sky
dark with night.

Have you ever seen
the moon out when
the sun shines bright?

Did the day moon
fade faint as a feather
in the sunshiny blue sky?

Have
you ever
seen the
silver moon's
sliver-curved
arm bent
with its
elbow
sticking
out?

8

Have you ever seen a huge,
yellow moon peek above
the eastern horizon
as the sun sets
in the west?

Did the yellow moon
pale to white
and look smaller
as it made its way
up the sky that night?

Did the whole,
full moon
shine its bright,
grand self
in the big, big sky
all through
the night?

Have you ever seen a high-sky moon
when a cloud crowd
scoots across the dark sky?

Did the high-sky moon get blocked when a cloud crowd stopped?

Have you ever seen a star-strewn sky
and not spy the moon out
in plain sight?

Did the star-strewn sky make
a no-moon-tonight
night?

Wherever
we live in our
wonderful world,
if we look all around
our peekaboo moon
can usually
be found.

Have YOU ever looked up at the sky and wondered **where in the world is the MOON?**

RESOURCE GUIDE
for *Where in the World is the Moon?*

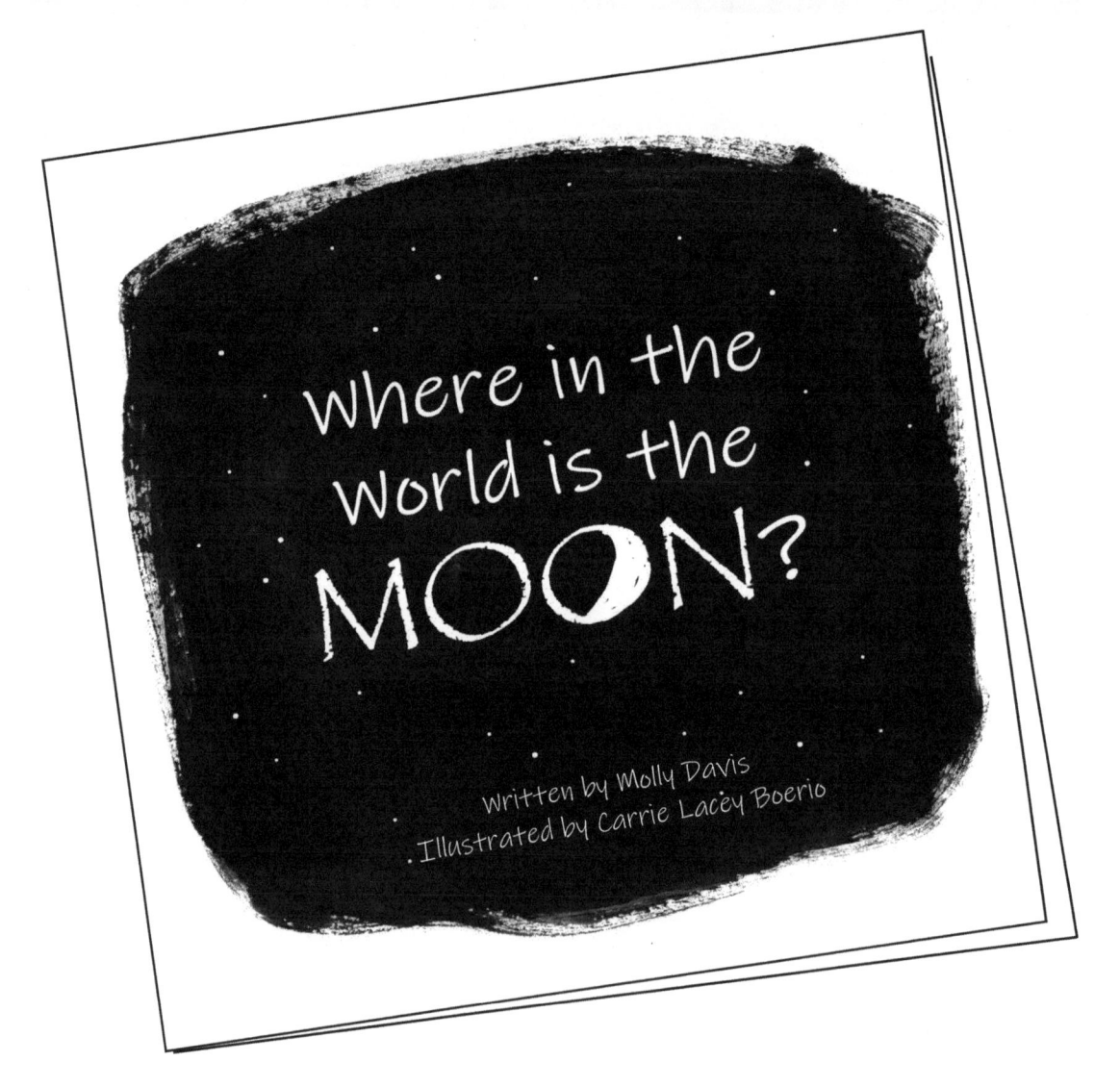

Where in the World is the MOON?

Written by Molly Davis
Illustrated by Carrie Lacey Boerio

Developed by Denise V. Carskadon and Anne C. Albrecht

This resource guide, developed to supplement *Where in the World is the Moon?*, can be used as a learning tool for any other children's book about Earth's moon. The guide supports teachers, librarians, homeschoolers, and parents of students in kindergarten through second grade.

The guide offers ideas and activities to integrate *Where in the World is the Moon?* or other children's books about Earth's moon into English language arts (ELA), science, and related arts curricula.

CPSIA information can be obtained
at www.ICGtesting.com
Printed in the USA
LVHW071516231121
703954LV00008B/27